MW01205785

Jesus Is King

JAKE & KEITH PROVANCE

WORD & SPIRIT
PUBLISHING

Jesus Is King
ISBN: 978-1-949106-27-5
Copyright © 2019 by Word and Spirit Publishing

Published by Word and Spirit Publishing
P.O. Box 701403
Tulsa, Oklahoma 74170
wordandspiritpublishing.com

Contents

"You say correctly that I am a King.
This is why I was born, and for this I
have come into the world."

−JESUS

{John 18:37 AMP}

Jesus Is King

Jesus is the King of kings and the Lord of lords. He is the Son of God, who sits at the right hand of God and reigns in majesty on high. The living Savior who died for you and me. Who defeated Satan, and reconciled man back to God. Who set us free from sin, a gruesome destiny, and a pitiful existence. Jesus Himself said:

"As I live, says the Lord, every knee shall bow to Me, and every tongue shall confess to God [acknowledge Him to His honor and to His praise]. And so each of us shall give an account of himself [give an answer in reference to judgment] to God."

—ROMANS 14:11-12 (AMPC)

Jesus is King, and all will come to realize this fact—if not now, then eventually, but we have a wonderful opportunity to express our faith in this life by declaring Him King! So many people shirk away from the idea that they should submit to Jesus as King and the Bible as the final authority, because they don't want to give up their position as ruler over their own life. If they only understood why Jesus wants to be their King.

He wants to protect us. He wants to lead us toward a bright future. Ultimately, He wants to spend eternity with us in His kingdom! When the Bible tells us what to do, it has nothing to do with us proving our piety or devotion by self-sacrifice, it's because Jesus knows what we need to live the most satisfying and fulfilling life possible, and He desires it for you!

Do you trust that Jesus has your best interest at heart? Then declare Him as your King and choose to live your life according to His Word. There can only be one King of your life, either you will continue to live the way you desire, determine right and wrong for yourself, and maintain control over what you will do, or you will believe that Jesus has your best interest at heart. Declare Him as your King, follow the example He set, and accept the Bible as truth and the final authority in your life. Once Jesus becomes your King, you will experience joy unspeakable, a peace that passes all understanding, a partnership that will cause you to walk through life confidently, with your head held high, infused by His strength. Jesus is King, and the King has your back!

Scriptures

So Pilate said to Him, "Then You are a King?" Jesus answered, "You say [correctly] that I am a King. This is why I was born, and for this I have come into the world, to testify to the truth. Everyone who is of the truth [who is a friend of the truth and belongs to the truth] hears and listens carefully to My voice."

–JOHN 18:37 (AMP)

I'm charging you before the life-giving God and before Christ, who took his stand before Pontius Pilate and didn't give an inch: Keep this command to the letter, and don't slack off. Our Master, Jesus Christ, is on his way. He'll show up right on time, his arrival guaranteed by the Blessed and Undisputed Ruler, High King, High God. He's the only one death can't touch, his light so bright no one can get close. He's never been seen by human eyes—human eyes can't take him in! Honor to him, and eternal rule! Oh, yes.

–1 Tɪᴍᴏᴛʜʏ 6:13-16 (MSG)

They will go to war against the Lamb but the Lamb will defeat them, proof that he is Lord over all lords, King over all kings, and those with him will be the called, chosen, and faithful."

–Rᴇᴠᴇʟᴀᴛɪᴏɴ 17:14 (MSG)

Then the final stage of completion comes, when he will bring to an end every other rulership, authority, and power, and he will hand over his kingdom to Father God. Until then he is destined to reign as King until all hostility has been subdued and placed under his feet. And the last enemy to be subdued and eliminated is death itself.

–1 Cᴏʀɪɴᴛʜɪᴀɴs 15:24-26 (TPT)

God, my God, omnipotent King, I humbly
adore thee. Thou art King of kings, Lord of
lords. Thou art the Judge of every age. Thou
art the Redeemer of souls. Thou art the
Liberator of those who believe. Thou art the
Hope of those who toil. Thou art the
Comforter of those in sorrow. Thou art the
Way to those who wander. Thou art Master to
the nations. Thou art the Creator of all creatures. Thou art the Lover of all good. Thou art
the Prince of all virtues. Thou art the joy of all
Thy saints. Thou art life perpetual. Thou art
joy in truth. Thou art the exultation in the
eternal fatherland. Thou art the Light of light.
Thou art the Fountain of holiness. Thou art
the glory of God the Father in the height.
Thou art Savior of the world. Thou art the
plenitude of the Holy Spirit. Thou sittest at
the right hand of God the Father on the
throne, reigning for ever.

–St. Patrick

"I am he that lives, and was dead; and,
behold, I am alive for evermore."

–JESUS

{Revelation 1:18}

Jesus Is Risen

The resurrection of Jesus Christ is the cornerstone belief that defines Christianity and separates it from all other religions. What other religion can claim their patriarch rose from the dead? None. God's immeasurable power and fathomless love for us was put on display for the world to see through raising up Christ from the grave, from spiritual destitution, and from Hell. His resurrection was the final confirmation He was truly the Son of God. God ripped Jesus from the clutches of death, and when Jesus rose from the dead He broke the power of death. Later, when Jesus appeared to one of His disciples, He proclaimed, "I am the living one—and behold I am alive forevermore and I hold the keys to death and hell."

It was not enough for Jesus just to die on the cross for our sins. His resurrection sealed the deal! His resurrection established His position as King of kings and Lord of lords, sitting at the right hand of God for all eternity. The Bible also tells us this amazing fact: that God has made that same resurrection power available to all believers.

"The Spirit of God, who raised Jesus from the dead, lives in you. And just as God raised Christ Jesus from the dead, he will give life to your mortal bodies by this same Spirit living within you."

–ROMANS 8:11 (NLT)

The same power that was in Christ—that caused him to rise up out of the grave—lives in you. All you have to do is tap into it. Plug into that Spirit of power inside you. Walk with a confident expectation that you will rise out of your depression. That you will rise out of your anxiety. That you will rise out of your social and financial standing. That you will rise out of your poor education. That you will rise out of your family's mistakes. That you will rise out of any and every situation that dares to try to keep you bound. Because Jesus rose, we can rise! That is the true power of His resurrection. Life-altering power echoed out into all of eternity from the defining moment that was Christ's ascension. And that same power resonates within us the moment we release our faith and act upon the truth within His Word. So rise, for Jesus is risen!

Scriptures

But God, who is rich in mercy, for his great love wherewith he loved us, Even when we were dead in sins, hath quickened us together with Christ, (by grace ye are saved;) And hath raised us up together, and made us sit together in heavenly places in Christ Jesus: That in the ages to come he might shew the exceeding riches of his grace in his kindness toward us through Christ Jesus.

–EPHESIANS 2:4-7

Christ's resurrection is your resurrection too. This is why we are to yearn for all that is above, for that's where Christ sits enthroned at the place of all power, honor, and authority!

–COLOSSIANS 3:1 (TPT)

And as to His divine nature according to the Spirit of holiness was openly designated the Son of God in power in a striking, triumphant and miraculous manner by His resurrection from the dead, even Jesus Christ our Lord (the Messiah, the Anointed One).

–ROMANS 1:4 (AMPC)

Yes, God raised Jesus to life! And since God's Spirit of Resurrection lives in you, he will also raise your dying body to life by the same Spirit that breathes life into you!

–ROMANS 8:11 (TPT)

Arise from the depression and prostration in which circumstances have kept you—rise to a new life! Shine (be radiant with the glory of the Lord), for your light has come, and the glory of the Lord has risen upon you!

–ISAIAH 60:1 (AMPC)

For the light makes everything visible. This is why it is said, "Awake, O sleeper, rise up from the dead, and Christ will give you light."

–EPHESIANS 5:14 (NLT)

Oh, eternal and everlasting God, direct my thoughts, words and work. Wash away my sins in the immaculate blood of the Lamb and purge my heart by Thy Holy Spirit. Daily, frame me more and more in the likeness of Thy son, Jesus Christ, that living in Thy fear, and dying in Thy favor, I may in thy appointed time obtain the resurrection of the justified unto eternal life. Bless, O Lord, the whole race of mankind and let the world be filled with the knowledge of Thee and Thy son, Jesus Christ.

–GEORGE WASHINGTON

"If you abide in me, and my words abide in you, ask whatever you wish, and it will be done for you."

–JESUS

{John 15:7 ESV}

Jesus Is Our Advocate

After His resurrection, the Bible tells us that Jesus ascended back to heaven and He took His place at the right hand of God. He now lives to make intercession for us. Jesus is praying for you right now, how cool is that! He has become your Advocate.

An advocate is, "a person who pleads on someone else's behalf." Your Advocate is revealed in 1 John 2:1 (NLT), *"My dear children, I am writing this to you so that you will not sin. But if anyone does sin, we have an advocate who pleads our case before the Father. He is Jesus Christ, the one who is truly righteous."* Your prayers don't have to be perfect because Jesus is, and when He hears what you're saying, He takes your part and pleads your case to God for you. It's a sweet transition, because Jesus knows precisely what you are going through. The

Bible even says, *"For we do not have a High Priest who is unable to sympathize and understand our weaknesses and temptations, but One who has been tempted knowing exactly how it feels to be human in every respect as we are, yet without committing any sin."* (Hebrews 4:15 AMP).

That means He knows exactly what you are feeling and wants to help you. Who else can claim that they love you so much that they died for you? Before many of the miracles Jesus performed, the Bible notes that He had compassion for the people. Jesus loves you and feels the pain you've been going through. Which means if you are sincere and honest towards God, and you are seeking help in any area, then Jesus is going to take up your case. You don't have to be a super Christian, knowing every scripture in the Bible and living perfectly. In fact, you don't have to do a single thing to make your request a reality except believe on Jesus. Jesus takes care of the rest. Don't worry, don't be afraid, trust in Jesus. Let Him help

you, even if you have messed up big time—
there is no sin so big, no mistake so bad, that
is greater than Jesus' love and sacrifice. So,
talk to your advocate, pour out your heart
concerning any and everything, rather it be
big or small, and don't let go of your faith in
Him for one second!

Scriptures

*For there is one God, and one mediator
between God and men, the man Christ Jesus.*

–1 TIMOTHY 2:5

*For Christ has entered, not into holy places
made with hands, which are copies of the true
things, but into heaven itself, now to appear in
the presence of God on our behalf.*

–HEBREWS 9:24 (ESV)

*Just think how much more the blood of
Christ will purify our consciences from sinful
deeds so that we can worship the living God.
For by the power of the eternal Spirit, Christ
offered himself to God as a perfect sacrifice for*

our sins. That is why he is the one who mediates a new covenant between God and people, so that all who are called can receive the eternal inheritance God has promised them. For Christ died to set them free from the penalty of the sins they had committed under that first covenant.

–Hebrews 9:14-15 (NLT)

Who is he that condemneth? It is Christ that died, yea rather, that is risen again, who is even at the right hand of God, who also maketh intercession for us.

–Romans 8:34

Wherefore he is able also to save them to the uttermost that come unto God by him, seeing he ever liveth to make intercession for them.

–Hebrews 7:25

My dear children, I write this to you so that you will not sin. But if anybody does sin, we have an advocate with the Father—Jesus Christ, the Righteous One.

–1 John 2:1 (NIV)

By opening our lives to God in Christ, we become new creatures. This experience, which Jesus spoke of as the new birth, is essential if we are to be transformed nonconformists . . . Only through an inner spiritual transformation do we gain the strength to fight vigorously the evils of the world in a humble and loving spirit.

–MARTIN LUTHER KING JR.

"I am the way, the truth, and the life: no man comes unto the Father, but by me."

–JESUS

{John 14:6}

Jesus Is the Way

Many people say there are multiple paths that lead to God, and through a journey of self-discovery you can find your own way to God. This belief is a lie. There is only one way that leads to God, and His name is Jesus. Jesus is the way—not just a way, but the *only* way. There is only one way that we get to spend eternity in heaven, there is only one way that we get to enjoy a relationship with the Father God that transcends this life into the next. There is only one way, and His name is Jesus.

Jesus took the punishment for all our sins and opened the door for us to commune with the Father. So that we could overcome every adversity in life, He made a way for us to become new creatures! He made a way for us to assume new identities. He made a way for our destinies to be rewritten. We were once fated for a life of pain, destined for the inevitable conclusion of our sins and misdeeds: death. But now we are fated for a life full of joy, peace, purpose, and fulfillment, with the conclusion of our journey: spending eternity in Heaven with a loving Father.

Jesus is the way, He is the avenue by which we communicate with the Father, He is the identity that was placed in us. It was His title that was placed on us, and His peace infused within us. It was His choice that gave us a choice. You may feel like you have messed up so badly that you will never enjoy life again. You may feel like you have dug a hole so deep that you can never find a way out, that all your hope for a better life is gone. You may feel confused. You may feel lost. You may even feel stuck, with your regrets, worries, and helplessness acting as a tomb for your hopes and dreams. If this describes you, then congratulations! You are about to introduce your hopeless situation to the Way-maker. Jesus specializes in making a way for His people when there seems to be no way. He is the master of doing the impossible for His kids. He is the way out of your situation—believe that, trust that He has your back, and watch as Jesus makes a way just for you.

Scriptures

Jesus saith unto him, I am the way, the truth, and the life: no man cometh unto the Father, but by me.

–JOHN 14:6

Thus saith the Lord, which maketh a way in the sea, and a path in the mighty waters.

–ISAIAH 43:16

"For this is how God loved the world: He gave his uniquely existing Son so that everyone who believes in him would not be lost but have eternal life. Because God sent the Son into the world, not to condemn the world, but that the world would be saved through him.

–JOHN 3:16-17 (ISV)

Our faith in Jesus transfers God's right-eousness to us and he now declares us flawless in his eyes. This means we can now enjoy true and lasting peace with God, all because of what our Lord Jesus, the Anointed One, has done for us. Our faith guarantees us permanent access into this marvelous kindness that has given us a perfect relationship with God. What incredible joy bursts forth within us as we keep on celebrating our hope of experiencing God's glory!

–ROMANS 5:1-2 (TPT)

By his death, Jesus opened a new and life-giving way through the curtain into the Most Holy Place.

–HEBREWS 10:20 (NLT)

Trust in the Lord with all your heart; do not depend on your own understanding. Seek his will in all you do, and he will show you which path to take.

–PROVERBS 3:5-6 (NLT)

You will show me the way of life, granting me the joy of your presence and the pleasures of living with you forever.

–PSALM 16:11 (NLT)

Make sure of your commitment to Jesus Christ, and seek to follow Him every day. Don't be swayed by the false values and goals of this world, but put Christ and His will first in everything you do.

–Billy Graham

"If you continue in my word, then you are my disciples indeed; And you shall know the truth, and the truth shall make you free."

–Jesus

{John 8:31-32}

Jesus Is the Truth

Looking at society today, it would seem like it is void of any definite moral compass, as if there is no such thing as black and white anymore. Right and wrong, honor and truth seem to have become relative terms defined by each individual's belief system. But truth is not relative, morality is not gray, and honor is still achieved by choosing right instead of wrong. And yet society still seeks to drag many down to their level of confusion produced through the degradation of morality and truth.

After all, how can one live a fulfilled life without foundational truth to build upon, without morality as boundaries, and without something to build towards like honor? Truth is not a myth, and it is not relative; truth is Jesus. And Jesus, according to the Bible, is the Word of God incarnate. The Bible is truth. Truth is not subjective, it is not like beauty, "in the eye of the beholder," it is finite, unchanging, and incorruptible. Time cannot erode it, cultures cannot bend it, and reasoning cannot alter its meaning. It is the way we are to live our lives. It shows us how we are to operate under every type of circumstance. It is our road map and guidebook to the fulfilled and satisfied life.

There are not many sources of truth, there is only one truth by which we can build our lives on and it is the Word of God. Don't endeavor to find a way to justify your belief system by adopting some human philosophy—establish your belief system on the truths and principles found in God's eternal Word. It is the cornerstone for the Christian walk, and the source of all that is good, honest, and pure in this life. To live according to Jesus' principles, to make His motivations your own, to make His character your own.

This should be our daily quest—to become imitators of Christ. Then we will find the fulfilled life full of peace, clarity, and a real joy of living. We must accept the Bible as truth. We must accept it as the final authority in our lives. We must judge everything in life by it, and endeavor to follow it. For when we follow truth, we follow Jesus, and we know that the Truth (Jesus) shall set us free!

Scriptures

Jesus said to the people who believed in him, "You are truly my disciples if you remain faithful to my teachings. And you will know the truth, and the truth will set you free."

–JOHN 8:31-32 (NLT)

In the beginning before all time was the Word (Christ), and the Word was with God, and the Word was God Himself. He was present originally with God. All things were made and came into existence through Him; and without Him was not even one thing made that has come into being. In Him was Life, and the Life was the Light of men.

–JOHN 1:1-4 (AMPC)

Jesus saith unto him, I am the way, the truth, and the life: no man cometh unto the Father, but by me.

–JOHN 14:6

"Your Word is truth! So make them holy by the truth."

—JOHN 17:17 (TPT)

Since by your obedience to the truth you have purified yourselves for a sincere love of the believers, see that you love one another from the heart always unselfishly seeking the best for one another, for you have been born again that is, reborn from above—spiritually transformed, renewed, and set apart for His purpose not of seed which is perishable but from that which is imperishable and immortal, that is, through the living and everlasting word of God.

—1 PETER 1:22-23 (AMP)

And the Word (Christ) became flesh (human, incarnate) and tabernacled (fixed His tent of flesh, lived awhile) among us; and we actually saw His glory (His honor, His majesty), such glory as an only begotten son receives from his father, full of grace (favor, loving-kindness) and truth.

—JOHN 1:14 (AMPC)

"It is a very good thing that you read the Bible... The Bible is Christ, for the Old Testament leads up to this culminating point... Christ alone... has affirmed as a principal certainty, eternal life, the infinity of time, the nothingness of death, the necessity and the raison d'être of serenity and devotion. He lived serenely, as a greater artist than all other artists, despising marble and clay as well as color, working in living flesh. That is to say, this matchless artist... made neither statues nor pictures nor books; he loudly proclaimed that he made... living men, immortals."

~Vincent van Gogh

"For if you choose self-sacrifice and lose your lives for my glory, you will continually discover true life. But if you choose to keep your lives for yourselves, you will forfeit what you try to keep. For even if you were to gain all the wealth and power of this world with everything it could offer you—at the cost of your own life— what good would that be? And what could be more valuable to you than your own soul?"

–Jesus

{Matthew 16:25-26 TPT}

Jesus Is the Life

Jesus said in John 10:10, *"I have come so that you may have life and have it more abundantly."* When you accept Jesus as your Savior, His life becomes infused into your own. The life Jesus is talking about is not just surviving a day to day bleak existence, but it is a vibrant, joyful adventure! So, what does it mean then to say that Jesus IS life? It means just that, before we accept Christ, we are the walking dead, unconsciously unaware of what we are missing and what we are working towards. Once saved, we are awakened from that existence, brought to life, raised up with Christ to the life that He came to give us—connected to the source of all life!

Accepting Jesus as our personal Lord and Savior opens the door for life to be breathed into us. Jesus gives purpose to our lives, but He doesn't stop there. He gives us supernatural peace, an overwhelming joy, a hope that supersedes any hardship, and the most intimate relationship that transcends this life on into the next. To live life without Jesus is to base your identity on what others think of you; to base your performance on promotion, and your success on power, wealth, or influence.

Many people chase after the things that they believe will bring them peace and happiness. But true peace and happiness can only be found in Jesus. No vacation can hold a candle to the peace of God, no job can provide the security and fulfillment that obedience to the Father can, no accolades from the world's most esteemed individuals can ever compare to the Lord's acceptance and approval. He knows you inside and out, all the good, the bad, and the ugly, and still loves you unconditionally and claims you as His kid!

The best thing you could ever do for yourself, for your spouse, for your kids, for your job, for every person in your life is to throw your whole self into a relationship with God. To serve Him wholeheartedly, and to lay down your old way of thinking, speaking, and living, and begin to imitate Christ! There is a life of fulfillment and joy for every believer who lives for the King. There is only one truly satisfied life—the life filled with Jesus.

Scriptures

"...I am the Resurrection, and I am Life Eternal. Anyone who clings to me in faith, even though he dies, will live forever. And the one who lives by believing in me will never die. Do you believe this?"

–JOHN 11:25(B)-26 (TPT)

Your old life is dead. Your new life, which is your real life—even though invisible to spectators—is with Christ in God. He is your life. When Christ (your real life, remember) shows up again on this earth, you'll show up, too—the real you, the glorious you. Meanwhile, be content with obscurity, like Christ.

–COLOSSIANS 3:3-4 (MSG)

Verily, verily, I say unto you, He that heareth my word, and believeth on him that sent me, hath everlasting life, and shall not come into condemnation; but is passed from death unto life.

–JOHN 5:24

Very truly I tell you, the one who believes has eternal life. I am the bread of life.

−JOHN 6:47-48 (NIV)

Even when we were dead (slain) by our own shortcomings and trespasses, He made us alive together in fellowship and in union with Christ; He gave us the very life of Christ Himself, the same new life with which He quickened Him, for it is by grace (His favor and mercy which you did not deserve) that you are saved (delivered from judgment and made partakers of Christ's salvation).

−EPHESIANS 2:5 (AMPC)

The thief cometh not, but for to steal, and to kill, and to destroy: I am come that they might have life, and that they might have it more abundantly.

−JOHN 10:10

This is the testimony in essence: God gave us eternal life; the life is in his Son. So, whoever has the Son, has life; whoever rejects the Son, rejects life.

−1 JOHN 5:11-12 (MSG)

No man can read the gospels
without feeling the actual presence
of Jesus. His personality pulsates in
every word. No myth is filled with
such life.

–ALBERT EINSTEIN

"Are you tired? Worn out? Burned out on religion? Come to me. Get away with me and you'll recover your life. I'll show you how to take a real rest. Walk with me and work with me—watch how I do it. Learn the unforced rhythms of grace. I won't lay anything heavy or ill-fitting on you. Keep company with me and you'll learn to live freely and lightly."

–JESUS

{Matthew 11:28-30 MSG}

Jesus Is for You

Jesus is for you; He is not against you. When you fail, He is for you. When you sin, He is for you. When you disobey, He is for you. When you ignore Him for years, He is still for you. When you feel like He is a million miles away, He is for you. God says you are the apple of His eye, and Jesus knew full well the mistakes you would make, the sins you would commit, and the wrong choices that you would make—and He still chose to pick up the cross just so you could always have the chance to be reunited with your heavenly Father.

With every flesh-ripping lash from the whip He received, with each nail that was driven into His body, with every thorn jammed into His scalp, with every agonizing step carrying the cross, and with each asphyxiating second He hung on the cross, He was thinking of you. It wasn't any nail, authority, or guard that held Him to the cross, it was love. He saw your life fated for pain and torment, and He willingly sacrificed Himself to spare you. He took your shame, He took your pain, He took your sin, He took your sickness, and ultimately, He took your place.

You were worth it to Him. That's why when you fail, disobey, fall short, and misprioritize things over Him, it doesn't change the way He sees you. If you did everything right, there would have never been a reason for the cross. He bore it all for your sake because He wants to see you happy, flourishing in life, fulfilled, successful, full of joy, full of peace, equipped with faith, armed with His Spirit, and ever ready to spread the good news about what Jesus did for you. You didn't earn this love, and it's doubtful that you will ever be able to fully understand His love this side of Heaven, but, you can accept that regardless of what you have done or will do, regardless of what you have said, or will say, regardless of what you have thought or will think, Jesus loves you and He is for you. He has plans to prosper you, to help you, to get you on your feet, to spend time with you and give you a glorious future. Believe it! Jesus is for you.

Scriptures

For we do not have a High Priest Who is unable to understand and sympathize and have a shared feeling with our weaknesses and infirmities and liability to the assaults of temptation, but One Who has been tempted in every respect as we are, yet without sinning. Let us then fearlessly and confidently and boldly draw near to the throne of grace (the throne of God's unmerited favor to us sinners), that we may receive mercy for our failures and find grace to help in good time for every need appropriate help and well-timed help, coming just when we need it.

–Hebrews 4:15-16 (AMPC)

Up to this time you have not asked a single thing in My Name as presenting all that I Am; but now ask and keep on asking and you will receive, so that your joy (gladness, delight) may be full and complete.

—JOHN 16:24 (AMPC)

Let them shout for joy, and be glad, that favour my righteous cause: yea, let them say continually, Let the Lord be magnified, which hath pleasure in the prosperity of his servant.

—PSALM 35:27

For God so loved the world, that he gave his only begotten Son, that whosoever believeth in him should not perish, but have everlasting life.

—JOHN 3:16

For I am persuaded, that neither death, nor life, nor angels, nor principalities, nor powers, nor things present, nor things to come, Nor height, nor depth, nor any other creature, shall be able to separate us from the love of God, which is in Christ Jesus our Lord.

—ROMANS 8:38-39

How priceless is your unfailing love, O God! People take refuge in the shadow of your wings.

—PSALM 36:7 (NIV)

"There is no pit so deep, that God's love is not deeper still."

–CORRIE TEN BOOM
(HOLOCAUST SURVIVOR)

"I am with you always, even to the end of the age."

–JESUS

{Matthew 28:20 NLT}

Jesus Is with You

The world has painted God as a stern taskmaster, sitting forbiddingly upon a throne looking down in disappointment upon everyone. And many have felt that the only way to escape the wrath of an indifferent God is by following a list of rules, having a plethora of good works, and giving up things like enjoyment and fun. To see Jesus in such a manner is to not see Jesus at all; it's akin to claiming Christianity as a mere religion that people adhere to instead of a personal relationship with Jesus Christ. When you accept Jesus as your personal Savior, you begin a relationship that will never end. Not even death can halt it.

After you accepted Jesus as your Savior, you became family, brothers and sisters with Him, able to enjoy His company as you would a dear friend. He promised us that He would never leave or forsake us. Regardless what you do or have done, regardless how many times you failed or will fail, and regardless of what challenges you might face, Jesus is still with you. He is ever ready to support, help, and undergird you. He is with you to give you strength to endure any hardship, to provide courage to overcome any challenge, and to provide comfort in times of sorrow. He is there to give you hope when your situation seems utterly hopeless. He is not sitting on a throne looking upon you in distain, He is with you, interceding for you, and if you let Him, enjoying every phase of your life with you.

Wisdom, guidance, answers to questions, and the best advice you could ever ask for is always within your reach if you but lean on Him and ask Him for it. Even when you fall short, not only does He stick it out through the tough times, through all of your mistakes, sins, and failures, He still never condemns, criticizes, or puts a guilt trip on you! Instead, He picks you up and dusts you off with a big smile on His face, and says, "I forgive you. Why don't you let me help you this time?"

Enjoy the elation, hope, peace, and guidance that was made available to you through a relationship with Jesus. Begin exploring the depths of His character through reading the Bible. Begin experiencing His love and His presence through worship. Begin letting Him become involved in every area of your life. Like all relationships, it takes time, but it will grow day by day and become the most rewarding experience in your entire life.

Scriptures

Yes, furthermore, I count everything as loss compared to the possession of the priceless privilege (the overwhelming preciousness, the surpassing worth, and supreme advantage) of knowing Christ Jesus my Lord and of progressively becoming more deeply and intimately acquainted with Him of perceiving and recognizing and understanding Him more fully and clearly. For His sake I have lost everything and consider it all to be mere rubbish (refuse, dregs), in order that I may win (gain) Christ (the Anointed One).

–PHILIPPIANS 3:8 (AMPC)

In conclusion, be strong in the Lord be empowered through your union with Him; draw your strength from Him that strength which His boundless might provides.

–EPHESIANS 6:10 (AMPC)

This is my command—be strong and courageous! Do not be afraid or discouraged. For the Lord your God is with you wherever you go."

–Joshua 1:9 (NLT)

Fear thou not; for I am with thee: be not dismayed; for I am thy God: I will strengthen thee; yea, I will help thee; yea, I will uphold thee with the right hand of my righteousness.

–Isaiah 41:10

…He God Himself has said, I will not in any way fail you nor give you up nor leave you without support. I will not, I will not, I will not in any degree leave you helpless nor forsake nor let you down (relax My hold on you!) Assuredly not!

–Hebrews 13:5(b) (AMPC)

Be strong and courageous. Do not be afraid or terrified because of them, for the Lord your God goes with you; he will never leave you nor forsake you.

–Deuteronomy 31:6 (NIV)

The Lord your God is with you, the Mighty Warrior who saves. He will take great delight in you; in his love he will no longer rebuke you, but will rejoice over you with singing.

–Zephaniah 3:17 (NIV)

"A rule I have had for years is: to treat the Lord Jesus Christ as a personal friend. His is not a creed, a mere doctrine, but it is He Himself we have."

–Dwight L. Moody

"I have revealed to them who you are and I will continue to make you even more real to them, so that they may experience the same endless love that you have for me, for your love will now live in them, even as I live in them!"

–JESUS

(PRAYING TO THE FATHER FOR US)

{John 17:26 TPT}

Jesus Is in You

When you became a Christian, Jesus came to live in you! The Bible tells us, *"For we are the temple of the living God. As God said: 'I will live in them and walk among them. I will be their God, and they will be my people,'"* 2 Corinthians 6:16 (NLT). Before Christ came, God's presence was held in temples and the ark of the covenant, and the only way we could communicate with Him was through a priest. But now, because of Jesus, we are washed clean, a pure vessel to house the living Spirit of Christ in us!

To say that Jesus is in you can sound confusing, as though it isn't quite clear what that even looks like. How can someone live in someone else? However, the scriptures lay it out for us. It means that everything that Jesus was, He now is, in you. His identity, His love, His peace, His wisdom, His joy, His passion to fulfill the will of God, and His intimacy with God were all implanted inside us the moment we became born again. We now have access to God as Jesus did, and God looks at us lovingly, as His very own kids, just as He looked at Jesus!

So why then do many Christians walk around as victims in life, void of any actionable evidence that Christ lives within us? Why isn't every child of God experiencing peace, joy, clarity, passion, and a real sense of identity? It's because though you have all of it, you haven't learned how to tap into it. It is like a light socket, it has power behind the wall, untapped, unseen. In order to tap into that power, you have to plug your cord into the socket. This is what we have to do with our faith! When you feel wearied, tap into Christ's unending reserve of strength. When you feel worried, stressed, or tired, tap into His peace that passes all understanding. When you need clarity, then tap into His wisdom and guidance! Whatever situation you are facing, Jesus is greater than it!

The Bible says in 1 John 4:4, *"greater is he that is in you, than he that is in the world."* He's greater than any storm that could come, He's greater than any crisis you could face, He's greater than any power that could come against you. It's the revelation of Christ in you that allows for the impactful life of every believer!

Scriptures

And Christ lives within you, so even though your body will die because of sin, the Spirit gives you life because you have been made right with God.

–ROMANS 8:10 (NLT)

I have revealed to them who you are and I will continue to make you even more real to them, so that they may experience the same endless love that you have for me, for your love will now live in them, even as I live in them!

–JOHN 17:26 (TPT)

There is a divine mystery—a secret surprise that has been concealed from the world for generations, but now it's being revealed, unfolded and manifested for every holy believer to experience. Living within you is the Christ who floods you with the expectation of glory! This mystery of Christ, embedded within us, becomes a heavenly treasure chest of hope filled with the riches of glory for his people, and God wants everyone to know it!

—COLOSSIANS 1:26-27 (TPT)

"Ye are of God, little children, and have overcome them: because greater is he that is in you, than he that is in the world."

—1 JOHN 4:4

Examine yourselves, to see whether you are in the faith. Test yourselves. Or do you not realize this about yourselves, that Jesus Christ is in you?—unless indeed you fail to meet the test!

—2 CORINTHIANS 13:5 (ESV)

"The more we let God take us over, the more truly ourselves we become – because He made us. He invented us. He invented all the different people that you and I were intended to be. . .It is when I turn to Christ, when I give up myself to His personality, that I first begin to have a real personality of my own."

–C.S. Lewis

"I leave the gift of peace with you—
my peace. Not the kind of fragile
peace given by the world, but my
perfect peace. Don't yield to fear or
be troubled in your hearts—instead,
be courageous!"

–JESUS

{John 14:27 TPT}

Jesus Is the Prince of Peace

The Bible tells us in the book of Isaiah, speaking of Jesus, *"and his name shall be called Wonderful, Counselor, Mighty God, Everlasting Father, Prince of Peace."* Isaiah 9:6 (AMP). Jesus told His disciples after His resurrection and right before He ascended to heaven, *"Peace I leave with you; My own peace I now give and bequeath to you. Not as the world gives do I give to you. Do not let your hearts be troubled, neither let them be afraid. Stop allowing yourselves to be agitated and disturbed; and do not permit yourselves to be fearful and intimidated and cowardly and unsettled."* John 14:27 (AMPC).

The Prince of Peace left the blissful serenity that He operated in to us. If we follow Jesus, we are following peace. The Bible even says peace acts as a guide!

"Let the peace of Christ the inner calm of one who walks daily with Him be the controlling factor in your hearts deciding and settling questions that arise." Colossians 3:15a (AMP). Peace is not an emotion, it's a state of being, a plane of existence in which the pressures and concerns of the world cannot reach you because you have given them over to God. No matter what's going on in our lives, when we put our trust in the Lord and cast all our cares on Him, His peace will keep our hearts and minds. We can remain calm and collected even in the most adverse circumstances. Jesus told us, "I have told you these things, so that in Me you may have perfect peace. In the world you have tribulation and distress and suffering, but be courageous, be confident, be undaunted, be filled with joy; I have overcome the world. My conquest is accomplished, My victory abiding," John 16:33 (AMP).

Peace is not the absence of problems; it is the state where a child of God is self-assured because of his faith in God. Which means you can be full of peace right in the middle of a major crisis. Your joy and peace of mind are never at the mercy of your circumstances. When you choose to look to God and trust Him to take care of you and sustain you, then the challenges of this life will cease to overwhelm you and His peace will bring you to a state of calmness and joy that can only come from Him.

Scriptures

For unto us a child is born, unto us a son is given: and the government shall be upon his shoulder: and his name shall be called Wonderful, Counsellor, The mighty God, The everlasting Father, The Prince of Peace.

–ISAIAH 9:6

Let the peace of Christ the inner calm of one who walks daily with Him be the controlling factor in your hearts deciding and settling questions that arise. To this peace indeed you were called as members in one body of believers. And be thankful to God always.

–COLOSSIANS 3:15 (AMP)

Do not be anxious or worried about anything, but in everything every circumstance and situation by prayer and petition with thanksgiving, continue to make your specific requests known to God. And the peace of God that peace which reassures the heart, that peace which transcends all understanding, that peace which stands guard over your hearts and your minds in Christ Jesus is yours.

—PHILIPPIANS 4:6-7 (AMP)

Thou wilt keep him in perfect peace, whose mind is stayed on thee: because he trusteth in thee.

—ISAIAH 26:3

Depart from evil, and do good; seek peace, and pursue it.

—PSALM 34:14

The Lord will give strength unto his people; the Lord will bless his people with peace.

—PSALM 29:11

Those who love your instructions have great peace and do not stumble.

—PSALM 119:165 (NLT)

Give thanks to the baby asleep in the hay,
For it's Jesus Who gave us our first
    Christmas Day.
A king in disguise, God sent Him to men,
Revealed to our hearts, He comes again.

Lord of the galaxies as well as our earth,
A hymn of the Universe celebrates His birth.
He gives us His Spirit, His kingdom's within,
His peace can be ours by believing in Him.

His truth is a flame that ignites young souls,
He is comfort to men for whom the bell tolls,
He restores an image both marred and
    grown dim,
He's a constant wonder to those who
    love Him.

–LAVERNE RILEY O'BRIEN

"Love the Lord your God with all your heart and with all your soul and with all your mind. This is the first and greatest commandment. And the second is like it: Love your neighbor as yourself."

–JESUS

{Matthew 22:37-39 NIV}

Jesus Is Your Neighbor

Did you know that Jesus is your neighbor? You read it right, Jesus takes it personally when you are kind to your fellow man. Read it for yourself:

"'For I was hungry, and you gave Me something to eat; I was thirsty, and you gave Me something to drink; I was a stranger, and you invited Me in; I was naked, and you clothed Me; I was sick, and you visited Me with help and ministering care; I was in prison, and you came to Me ignoring personal danger.' Then the righteous will answer Him, 'Lord, when did we see You hungry, and feed You, or thirsty, and give You something to drink? And when did we see You as a stranger, and invite You in, or naked, and clothe You? And when did we see You sick, or in prison, and come to You?' The King will answer and say to them, 'I assure you and most solemnly say to you, to the extent that

*you did it for one of these brothers of Mine,
even the least of them, you did it for Me.'"*

–MATTHEW 25:35-40 (AMP)

As a Christian, our interactions with
others should be representative of the love of
God in us. Imagine if every Christian began
treating their neighbors as they would Jesus.
Jesus gave His disciples this very same direc-
tion in Matthew when He said: "Don't begin
by traveling to some far-off place to convert
unbelievers. And don't try to be dramatic by
tackling some public enemy. Go to the lost,
confused people right here in the neighbor-
hood." (Matthew 10:5-6 MSG)

If we are not careful, we can get so
wrapped up in our own lives that we develop
a selfish lifestyle. One small act of kindness—a sympathetic ear, a smile, or a kind
word—can have a powerful impact on
someone's life. It can open the door for
Christ's love to shine through you. If you
love Jesus, and you appreciate all that He's
done for you, and you think to yourself, "I
wish there was something that I could do for

Him in return," show kindness towards those who He died to save, treat them with respect, dignity, honor, and love, lend a helping hand, reach out to those less fortunate than you. Even the smallest amount of generosity can make a big difference. When you bless your neighbor, you are blessing Jesus!

Scriptures

And whoever gives to one of these little ones [in rank or influence] even a cup of cold water because he is My disciple, surely I declare to you, he shall not lose his reward.

–MATTHEW 10:42 (AMPC)

By this everyone will know that you are My disciples, if you have love and unselfish concern for one another.

–JOHN 13:35 (AMP)

And be ye kind one to another, tender-hearted, forgiving one another, even as God for Christ's sake hath forgiven you.

–EPHESIANS 4:32

Be kindly affectioned one to another with brotherly love; in honour preferring one another.

–ROMANS 12:10

So in everything, do to others what you would have them do to you, for this sums up the Law and the Prophets.

–MATTHEW 7:12 (NIV)

Do to others as you would have them do to you.

–LUKE 6:31 (NIV)

For all the law is fulfilled in one word, even in this; Thou shalt love thy neighbour as thyself.

–GALATIANS 5:14

This is my commandment, That ye love one another, as I have loved you.

–JOHN 15:12

Lord, make me an instrument of your peace:
where there is hatred, let me sow love;
where there is injury, pardon;
where there is doubt, faith;
where there is despair, hope;
where there is darkness, light;
where there is sadness, joy.
O divine Master, grant that I may not so
much seek to be consoled as to console,
to be understood as to understand,
to be loved as to love.
For it is in giving that we receive,
it is in pardoning that we are pardoned,
and it is in dying that we are born to
eternal life.
Amen.

–Prayer of St Francis of Assisi

"I am the resurrection, and the life: he that believes in me, though he were dead, yet shall he live."

–JESUS

{John 11:25}

Jesus Is Our Savior

Someone must pay. This one notion—a cry for justice to be served—is why every society, regardless how primitive, has some form of judicial system. The need for justice is why we see grieving people looking for somebody to blame, and why others carry immeasurable guilt and shame for past mistakes—as though their suffering will atone for their misdeeds.

It is a fact that our actions have consequences. We all deserve a miserable existence and no amount of trying to make up for our mistakes could ever come close to wiping our slates clean. The truth is, somebody truly must pay for all the sin and selfish acts that you and I have committed. Justice must be served, and through Jesus' death, justice was served, and somebody did pay.

One person, Adam, brought sin and suffering into the world when he disobeyed

God and ate the forbidden fruit. So God devised a plan to save us from a life fated for pain and suffering. He would need someone who was perfect in every way, to be tempted just as we are and yet remain faithful, to offer up Himself as our substitute. That sinless, perfect, loving person was Jesus. He became that sacrifice, the one chosen to suffer the shame, guilt, and reproach for our sins. To receive the judgment of God for the sins of all humanity. He did not come to punish the world, but to be punished for the world. All we have to do to receive the removal of all our sin, is to accept Jesus as our substitute, our Savior.

The Bible tells us:

"If you openly declare that Jesus is Lord and believe in your heart that God raised him from the dead, you will be saved. For it is by believing in your heart that you are made right with God, and it is by openly declaring your faith that you are saved. As the Scriptures tell us, 'Anyone who trusts in him will never be disgraced.'"

—ROMANS 10:9-11 (NLT)

Isn't that good news?! All of the pressure is off. You don't have to earn your salvation by trying to atone for your sins or by trying to live a perfect life. No amount of good works or penitence can atone for your sins. It is God's gift to you, bought and paid for by the blood of Jesus Christ. He truly is the Savior!

Scriptures

It is for this that we labor and strive often called to account, because we have fixed our confident hope on the living God, who is the Savior of all people, especially of those who believe in Him, recognize Him as the Son of God, and accept Him as Savior and Lord.

—1 TIMOTHY 4:10 (AMP)

You had Jesus arrested and killed by crucifixion, but the God of our forefathers has raised him up. He's the one God has exalted and seated at his right hand as our Savior and Champion. He is the provider of grace as the Redeemer of Israel.

—ACTS 5:30-31 (TPT)

But is now made manifest by the appearing of our Saviour Jesus Christ, who hath abolished death, and hath brought life and immortality to light through the gospel.

—2 TIMOTHY 1:10

Could it be any clearer? Our old way of life was nailed to the cross with Christ, a decisive end to that sin-miserable life—no longer at sin's every beck and call! What we believe is this: If we get included in Christ's sin-conquering death, we also get included in his life-saving resurrection. We know that when Jesus was raised from the dead it was a signal of the end of death-as-the-end. Never again will death have the last word. When Jesus died, he took sin down with him, but alive he brings God down to us. From now on, think of it this way: Sin speaks a dead language that means nothing to you; God speaks your mother tongue, and you hang on every word. You are dead to sin and alive to God. That's what Jesus did.

–ROMANS 6:6-11 (MSG)

If you would like to accept Jesus as your Savior right now, you can do that by praying this out loud, from your heart:

"Father, I have sinned and fallen short of your glory. I've made many mistakes, and I know that nothing I do could ever make up for all the sins I've committed. But, I do know that Jesus, acting as my substitute, took all my sin upon Himself on the cross and paid the price for it in full with His death and resurrection. I believe He was raised from the dead and sits right next to you, at your right hand making intercession for me. Jesus, I know you love me. I thank you for going through all that you did for my sake. I ask you to forgive me of all my sins and come into my heart. I now declare Jesus is my Lord and Savior. Thank you, for saving me. Amen.

If you have prayed this prayer for the first time, or to recommit your life to the one true King, congratulations, and welcome to the family!

About the Authors

Keith Provance, involved in Christian publishing for more than 40 years, is the founder and president of Word and Spirit Publishing, a company dedicated to the publishing and world-wide distribution of scriptural, life-changing books. He also works as a publishing consultant to national and international ministries. Keith continues to write with his wife and with his son Jake. He and his wife, Megan, have authored a number of bestselling books with total sales of over 2 million copies. They reside in Tulsa, Oklahoma and are the parents of three sons, Ryan, Garrett, and Jake.

You may contact Keith at
Keith@WordAndSpiritPublishing.com

Jake Provance is a successful young writer, who has written seven books and has plans to write several more. Jake's first book, Keep Calm & Trust God, has sold more than 600,000 copies. Jake is a graduate of Domata Bible School in Tulsa, OK, and has a call on his life to work in pastoral care ministry, with a particular passion to minister to young adults. Jake and his wife, Leah, live in Tulsa, OK.

You may contact Jake at
Jake@WordAndSpiritPublishing.com

Other inspirational books by Jake & Keith Provance

Keep Calm & Trust God - Volume 1

Keep Calm & Trust God - Volume 2

Keep Calm
(hardback gift edition - includes volumes 1&2)

Let Not Your Heart be Troubled

Scriptural Prayers for Victorious Living

I Am What the Bible Says I Am

I Have What the Bible Says I Have

I Can Do What the Bibles Says I Can Do